Contents

Taking turns

We take turns on the slide.

Me and y Frie

I Can Take Turns

written by Daniel Nunn

illustrated by Clare Elsom

raintree
a Capstone company — publishers for children

Raintree is an imprint of Capstone Global Library Limited,
a company incorporated in England and Wales having
its registered office at 7 Pilgrim Street, London, EC4V 6LB –
Registered company number: 6695582

www.raintreepublishers.co.uk
myorders@raintreepublishers.co.uk

Edited by Brynn Baker
Designed by Steve Mead and Kyle Grenz
Production by Helen McCreath
Original illustrations © Clare Elsom
Originated by Capstone Global Library Ltd
Printed and bound in China by LEO

ISBN 978 1 406 28164 4 (hardback)
18 17 16 15 14
10 9 8 7 6 5 4 3 2 1

ISBN 978 1 406 28169 9 (paperback)
19 18 17 16 15
10 9 8 7 6 5 4 3 2 1

British Library Cataloguing in Publication Data
A full catalogue record for this book is available from
the British Library.

Now it is my turn!

We take turns on the sledge.

Now it is my turn!

We take turns on the piano.

Now it is my turn!

We take turns on the tablet.

Now it is my turn!

We take turns at the shop.

Now it is my turn!

We take turns at the sink.

Now it is my turn!

We take turns with the dice.

Now it is my turn!

We take turns with the skipping rope.

Now it is my turn!

Taking turns quiz

Which of these pictures shows taking turns?

Did taking turns make these children happy? Why? What happens if you don't take turns?

Picture glossary

dice small cubes, marked with one to six dots used to play games

take turns to do something, one person after another, so that everyone gets to have a go

skipping rope a game where you swing a rope and jump over it

Index

Notes for teachers and parents

BEFORE READING

Building Background: Ask children what it means to take turns. When do they take turns? What can happen if they don't take turns?

AFTER READING

Recall and reflection: Ask the class how the children in the book took turns. (Waiting to wash, sharing the tablet.) What are some other activities you've had to take turns doing?

Sentence knowledge: Which punctuation mark is at the end of the sentence on page 5? (Exclamation mark.) How does the exclamation mark help us know how to read the sentence?

Word knowledge (phonics): Ask children point to the word *slide* on page 4. Sound out the three phonemes in the word *sl/ i/ de.* Ask children to sound out each phoneme as they point to the letters, and then blend the sounds together to make the word *slide.* What words rhyme with *slide*? (Glide, hide, ride.)

Word recognition: Ask the children to count how many times the words *turn/ turns* appear in the main text (not counting the quiz). (16)

AFTER-READING ACTIVITIES

Sing the following song to the tune "Frère Jacques" (or "Are You Sleeping").
First it's your turn. First it's your turn.
Then it's mine. Then it's mine.
We take turns and we share
That is fair. That is fair.

In this book

Topic
taking turns

Topic words and phrases
dice
my turn
piano
shop
sink
skipping rope
sledge
slide
tablet
take turns

Sentence stems
We ___ ___ on the __.
Then it is my ___ .
We ___ ___ with the ___.
We___ ___ at the ___ .

High-frequency words
at
is
it
my
now
on
the
we
with